YOU CAN LIVE THROUGH IT

A Life Interrupted

Foreword by
Pastor Renee Winston

By Vicky L. Richardson

YOU CAN LIVE THROUGH IT

A Life Interrupted

By Vicky L. Richardson

Copyright © 2021 by Vicky L. Richardson

ISBN: 978-1-955418-03-4

All rights reserved. No part of this book may be reproduced or used in any manner without written permission of the copyright owner except for the use of quotations in a book review.

Scriptures marked NKJV are taken from the NEW KING JAMES VERSION (NKJV): Scripture taken from the NEW KING JAMES VERSION®. Copyright© 1982 by Thomas Nelson, Inc. Used by permission. All rights reserved.

Scriptures marked KJV are taken from the KING JAMES VERSION (KJV): KING JAMES VERSION, public domain.

Scriptures marked MEV are taken from The Holy Bible, Modern English Version. Copyright © 2014 by Military Bible Association. Published and distributed by Charisma House.

PRAISE FOR "YOU CAN LIVE THROUGH IT"

Life is made up of seasons. Seasons of prosperity and seasons of lack, seasons of laughter and seasons of distress, seasons of healing and seasons of sickness. Ecclesiates 3:1 says, "To every thing there is a season and a time to every purpose under the heaven." But what happens when a season of lack, distress or sickness becomes long and arduous? In her memoir, You can live through it: A life interrupted, Vicky L. Richardson recounts her moments of despondency over a loss of a life once known and her acceptance of God's will.

In December 2011, Richardson's life was interrupted. That morning she suffered a devastating ischemic stroke that left her physically incapacitated. For ten years thereafter, Richardson had endured hospitalizations, sickness, and moments of depression and doubt. But God had a plan for her life.

As Richardson recounts her struggles, she lays bare the pain she felt through the most difficult time in her life. As I read her account I cried, not because I felt sorry for her, but because of her bravery, strength, and faith. Always wanting to root for the hero/heroine of any story, I found myself hoping and praying for God's restoration of Richardson to her once fully functioning self, not realizing until I read her memoir in its entirety, that God is using her for His divine assignment and for His glory. This becomes the central theme of her interrupted life.

While giving the reader the deep, down and dirty truth of her "Job experience," Richardson has a word of encouragement to those facing trials and tribulations, noting that there is truly a light at the end of a dark tunnel. This story, this word, this truth should be a required reading for anyone going through a struggle, for it not only tells a story, but gives the blueprint for overcoming.

You Can Live Through It: A life Interrupted is a brutally honest portrait of what happens when life brings pain and how God uses that pain for our good and His glory.

Rochelle Johnson Hendrix, M.Ed

Assistant principal

Vicky's riveting testimony inspires us all to know that not only can we live through the difficulties of life, but we can do so victoriously. "You Can Live Through It" is a must read for anyone who has had life interrupted by unpleasant events.

Mama Sue Roseberry

"Be Encouraged! ALL PROBLEMS HAVE AN EXPIRATION DATE!"

For many months you gave me this same encouragement during my own medical crisis. Many a day I have memories of you making me eat healthy after a disabling heart attack. The very first time I had avocado wheat toast for breakfast it was because you stood in my kitchen and made it. Notice I say, You stood… God had just spared me from the notorious, "Widow Maker" heart attack. As you helped me regain my ability to walk you were already noticeably in your own season of pain. Little did I know that you would soon have a debilitating stroke and begin your own "Walk into Life."

Your writing and words are so powerful that I give them

back to your readers.

You must have: UNSHAKABLE FAITH!!!

#1 BE UNSTOPPABLE!!!

#2 THE JOY OF THE LORD IS YOUR STRENGTH!

You will learn that God has created us to be UNSTOPPABLE!!!! In order for us to be unstoppable

#3 RELENTLESS FAITH!! We must have this…What is unstoppable and relentless faith?

It is a faith that is so focused and anchored in God and his word that THERE IS NO ROOM OR CHANCE OF DOUBT CREEPING IN AND YET TO BE MORE PRECISE SETTLING IN!!!

Hebrews 11:6) But WITHOUT FAITH it is impossible to please him: for he that cometh to God must believe that he is, and that he is a rewarder of them that diligently seek him.

Hebrews 1:1) NOW FAITH is the substance of things hoped for, the evidence of things not seen.

This is the heritage of the servants of the Lord, And their righteousness is from Me…

YOU ARE UNSTOPPABLE!!! Satan may knock you down but HE CANNOT KNOCK YOU OUT!!!

Why not? because Romans 16:20 declares,

And the God of peace will crush Satan under your feet SHORTLY!!!

HALLELUJAH!!! SHORTLY!!! HOLD ON, A CHANGE IS COMING!!!

This was a fast read, an enjoyable Spirit-filled Word from the Lord. IF YOU ARE STRUGGLING… spend an evening with this book and you will gain a new perspective.

"You Can Live Through It!"

Pastor Barbara Nutt-Duffey Hammonds

Tried In The Fire Ministries, Inc.

Table of Contents

Dedication

Preface

Foreword By Pastor Renee Winston

The Courage to Live Another Day.................................22

It Touched You, but Couldn't Take You........................29

It Hurt Me, But It Helped Me.......................................42

There's A Purpose In Your Pause.................................50

Rest In The Reset..54

Life As I Knew It: The Acceptance...............................63

My Life Isn't Over Yet..66

I Miss You, The Grieving Process................................70

Unshakeable Faith..73

Trials & Tribulations...77

Navigating Through The Unexpected.........................83

I Thank God For Yesterday..90

Embracing Your Life Now..96

The Life We Leave Behind...100

Restructuring Your Purpose..103

Facebook Posts..107

Encouraging Scriptures

Works Cited

Dedication

First, I want to give thanks to God for giving me the strength and energy to write this book to encourage everyone who reads it. I thank all my sisters Rose Jones, Gloria Williams, Loretta Andrews, Genetra (Gennie) Lewis, and Patricia Brown for their encouragement and support. Also, to my sisters from another mister, Sherri Adams, Susie Stancil, Carla Wright, Barbara A. Hammonds, and Omel Elliston for their prayers and support.

Thank you to my pastor Bishop Vernon R. Kemp and Lady Vicki L. Kemp you inspired me to write this book. I want to also thank Ashley Smith Witcher and The Write Legacy publishing company for helping me to deliver this book that I was pregnant with for years.

Arleana Frink-Waller, thank you for your support and encouragement. Pastor Renee Winston thank you for the beautiful foreword you wrote. Minister Sheryl Brown thank you for your support and encouragement. Thank you to Bishop Quacy Smith and the First 48 prayer partners for your prayers and encouragement.

Finally, I want to thank my nieces, nephews and two brothers-in-law Ronell and Wes. Last but definitely not least my late parents Freeman and Jennie Richardson for the stellar example they set while going through life's challenges when they were here. I dedicate this book to you all.

Preface

Life's challenges are inevitable, but they are not impossible to overcome. This journey we call life is filled with interruptions, distractions and even detours that are constantly competing for our attention as we make every effort to keep our eyes on Jesus. As you read this book, it is my deepest desire for you to come to the realization that you were designed by God to master life rather than life mastering you. In the latter half of I John 4:4 (KJV) it says, "Greater is he that is in you, than he that is in the world." Philippians 4:13 (KJV) says, "I can do all things through Christ which strengthens me." As you can see, God has placed His strength on the inside of us so we can overcome situations that arise in our lives. I have concluded that it is not so much the interruptions in life, but it is what you do in spite of the interruptions that determines whether you will be victorious or defeated.

After having a debilitating stroke, I found myself challenged not only physically, but also in my soul. My mind, will, and emotions were all in shock and on life support. My faith in God was challenged like never before. I was at the crossroads of faith and fear. One half of my body was paralyzed on the left side. And so was my faith. I questioned if I could trust God with this traumatic interruption. Can I live through this? The answer was and is a resounding yes! And so can you. *You Can Live Through It*!

Like me, you are not just meant to survive the interruption. Rather, you are meant to thrive and live while going through it. Some things that happen to us in life are over quickly, while others take a longer period of time to get through and overcome. It is during those times that we must hold on to the promises of God like never before! His word must permeate our souls during the most difficult times of our lives. It must cover and spread over our mind, will and emotions like a warm comforting blanket on a bitterly cold night.

"When I passed by you and saw you polluted in your own

blood, I said to you when you were in your blood, "Live!" Indeed, I said to you when you were in your blood, "Live!"

Ezekiel 16:6, MEV.

Foreword

By Pastor Renee Winston

"And they overcame him by the blood of the lamb and by the word of their testimony; and they loved not their lives unto death;" – Revelation 12:11. This is one of the most powerful scriptures in the Bible. Every time we share our testimony of victory and freedom from bondage, we grow stronger, we grow wiser and become better. Not only do we grow stronger, wiser and better, but we cause others to do the same. I have learned through the vicissitudes of life, that my struggle, my trials, my tribulations are not about me, but more so about who I will impact once I arrive to the place of my victory. The fact that

God "picks" us to be tested is powerful within itself. Out of all the people in the world, God would choose us to experience certain difficult trials and tribulations. Why does He do that? He does it because He trusts us. Yes, God trusts us to give Him all the glory in and out of the tests so that others may see and believe; not just see and believe, but also become followers of the Lord Jesus Christ. Our first commission once we are disciples/believers are to make more disciples.

In this most invigorating and inspiring book, "You Can Live Through It," the writer, Vicky Richardson, details and depicts for us her life journey through many ups and downs as it pertains to her health. Her story is a ready reminder that God is able to do exceeding and abundantly above all we can ask or think according to His power that works in us; Ephesians 3:20. Throughout her book, Ms. Richardson teaches us that what we fail to do many times is activate the power that lives on the inside of us. How is His power activated in us? The power is activated through our faith. Faith is what pleases God and draws Him closer to us. You will discover during this book that it is when our faith is demonstrated in our most difficult times that God's power on the inside of us is activated and the "mountain" can then be removed. In this book, you will see the many instances Vicky activated the power to conquer and not to merely survive. After reading this book, you will be encouraged and your faith will arise to a new dimension. You will be sure that it is God's desire that we conquer and not to survive. For to merely survive suggests that we barely made it. Each test that Ms. Richardson encountered she conquered in a greater fashion than one before. "You Can Live Through It" is more than a title, it is a "statement" to live by and an evident truth, through the life of Ms. Vicky Richardson.

Pastor Renee Winston

The Courage to Live Another Day

The two main points I want you to take away from this chapter are:

1. Live your life with purpose.

2. Always have the courage to move forward and not be inactive in your recovery process.

Do you remember your mother or grandmother having something of special significance in a designated place in the house? It may have been in the living room, bedroom, bathroom, or some other place in the house when you were a child, and you never forgot about it. That special something of significance for me is the "Serenity Prayer."

As early as I can remember, my mother had a plaque on the wall with the Serenity Prayer written on it. Before I learned to read, she read it to me. She gave so much life to everything she read; it was amazing! I was completely intrigued by this prayer because of the way Mama read it to me.

When I became old enough to attend school, I remembered this prayer. As I grew up, the Serenity Prayer helped to carry me through every difficulty in my life. Having a major stroke at only forty-three years old, which left me paralyzed and unable to walk or care for myself has proven to be the most challenging experience of my life. The waves of depression and thoughts of suicide held me captive for years. I give God all the glory for my life and for deliverance from the stronghold of major depression. At the time of writing this book, it will be ten years in December since it happened. I remember when I moved into this beautiful, yet cold and lonely facility eight years ago. I didn't come out of my room to participate in any of the activities for the first three months. I was completely devastated! My life had been reduced to me having to live in a place that was made for people who were my parents' and grandparents' ages.

One day after my therapy session, my physical therapist, Belinda, said, "I am not taking you back to your room now. You're going to bingo!" I was furious with her. She said," If you want to go back to your room, wheel yourself!" She knew I could not do that. I gave her the dirtiest look I could. Thankfully, it didn't work. She left me right there at the table in the activity room with all those strange, old people. As I looked around the room, I wondered what I had done to deserve this sentence. At the time, I was the youngest resident in the facility. I kept looking around, and all of a sudden, they started talking to me and smiling at me. Next, I was handed a bingo card and some markers. Then, I was introduced to everyone in the room by the activities assistant.

Slowly, my walls were coming down and being replaced with courage. I decided to participate and won a couple of games. Wow! I was finally able to have a littlfun and enjoy myself in this new reality. Some people say it's the new normal, but I choose to say a new reality. I needed something a little more "in your face." I finally began to embrace my new reality after staying in my room for the first three months of living in my new home.

After having so much fun that day, I decided to choose life. But the very next morning, I still needed strength to face another day in my new reality. I needed some courage to let them come and get me out of the bed again. I woke up to disappointment, again. No miraculous healing happened during the night, and I was still paralyzed and could not walk yet.

The Holy Spirit reminded me of the Serenity Prayer that Mama read to me when I was a little girl. I pressed the call button so my aide would come and get me ready for the day. I went to bingo and had another great time. I was living life again. Finally, I was seeing some light in this situation, and the Serenity Prayer gave me the encouragement I needed to know I could live through this new reality and so can you! *You Can Live Through It!*

Whatever difficulty you are facing right now, whatever

perplexing and depressing circumstances you are in are not enough to stop you. Whatever it is that caused you to pick up this book and start reading about how I am living through the absolute worst experience of my life has a purpose. *You can live through it* too. Hallelujah!

I implore you to know and understand that you can live through it. You can live again. You can have a meaningful life again. Receive this word right now in the name of Jesus. Hallelujah!

Dear one, this problem didn't catch God off guard or by surprise. He still has plans for your life. Jeremiah 29:11 in the New Living Translation has always been a favorite scripture for me: "For I know the plans I have for you," says the Lord. "They are plans for good and not for disaster, to give you a future and a hope."

Did you hear that? God says His plans are to give you a future and a hope! I pray that this book will give you the courage you need to live another day and to keep living. You are valuable and mighty in the eyes of God.

You Can Live Through It: A Life Interrupted

I hope that the Serenity Prayer will bless you in your major life interruption as much as it has blessed me. The Serenity Prayer could also be named the Peace Prayer. Since the definition of serenity is peace, I chose to say peace when I recited this prayer after my life changed so drastically. I start the prayer off like this, "God grant me the peace to accept the things I cannot change." This brings to my mind Philippians 4:7 that says, "And the peace of God, which surpasses all understanding, will guard your hearts and your minds in Christ Jesus" (ESV).

It has taken the peace of God to bring me to where I am today. After all these years living in a facility away from my family and missing out on so much of life with them, it has been the peace of God that has kept my heart and mind because when this first happened to me, I absolutely did not understand this chapter in my life. I give Him the praise, the glory, and the honor for deliverance from suicidal thoughts. Hallelujah! God is so faithful.

Because the Serenity Prayer has been such a powerful tool in my life, I'd like to share it with you.

Vicky L. Richardson

God, grant me the Serenity

To accept the things I cannot change;

Courage to change the things I can,

And Wisdom to know the difference.

Living one day at a time;

Enjoying one moment at a time;

Accepting hardship as the pathway to peace;

Taking, as He did, this sinful world

as it is,

Not as I would have it.

Trusting that He will make all things right

if I surrender to His will.

That I may be reasonably happy in this life.

And supremely happy with Him

forever in the next.

Amen.

Reinhold Niebuhr

"I can do all things through Christ who strengthens me"

You Can Live Through It: A Life Interrupted

(Philippians 4:13, NKJV).

Chapter 1 Reflections

Use this page to write down your thoughts. Did this chapter help you? If so, how?

_____
_____
_____
_____
_____
_____
_____

It Touched You But Couldn't Take You!

Let's talk about our brother, Apostle Paul. Particularly, let's look at his experience in Acts 27:22-25.

"Now I urge you to be encouraged. Not one of your lives will be lost, though we will lose the ship. Last night an angel from the God to whom I belong and whom I worship stood beside me. The angel said, 'Don't be afraid, Paul! You must stand before Caesar! Indeed, God has also graciously given you everyone to sail with you. Be encouraged, men! I have faith in God that it will be exactly as he told me."

Have faith in God. Paul had a divine assignment to speak

to Caesar. It had to be done. God was not going to allow Paul's present circumstances to destroy him before he finished what He planned for him to do. It's the same way for you and me. God will not allow this life interruption to destroy us! We must complete our divine assignments.

Don't live in fear because of this interruption in your life. Paul was obviously afraid that he wouldn't make it to his destination. We know this because in verse twenty-four, the angel told him not to be afraid. He had been wrongfully imprisoned for preaching the Gospel and was on a prison inmate ship out in the middle of the sea during what meteorologists today call a nor'easter. But Paul had strong faith after receiving the reassurance he needed that he would come out of that storm alive and fulfill his assignment. That kind of storm is known to be one of the most devastating. Life and property are almost always a guaranteed loss when caught in a nor'easter, unless like Paul, you are on a divine assignment.

That situation touched Paul, but it couldn't take him out because he had a divine assignment, to stand before Caesar.

Likewise, God will make sure that you fulfill whatever He has planned for you to do and to have in your life. Not only that, but others will also be delivered because of what you've gone through. Your testimony is vital to their victory! That's why it's crucial to live through your storm.

On December 5, 2011, at approximately 10:30 in the morning, I collapsed on the kitchen floor from an Ischemic stroke. I was immediately paralyzed on my left side and couldn't get up off the floor. I felt my mother's presence. She had passed away the previous year. I was in a peaceful state. Mama told me that I couldn't stay, and I had to go back. I said to her, "No, I want to stay here with you." She said, "You go back." I refused again. Next, my grandmother who we called "Big Mama" came over to me and got directly in my face and said, "You go back!" I said, "Okay, Big Mama." Immediately, I was back and fully aware of what happened to me. I heard my mother's voice say, "Crawl into the dining room and call out for Barbara."

Barbara was my roommate. I struggled and struggled until I was finally able to drag myself into the dining room. I screamed as loudly as I could, "Barbara!" She had woke up late and was rushing to get ready to go to work. I could hear her in the bathroom running water in the sink. She had no idea what had happened to me in the kitchen. Had she not been running late that day she would've in all probability come back home to a dead roommate. Thank God for divine delays. Glory hallelujah!

Barbara came out of the bathroom and as soon as she saw me, she knew I had a stroke. Immediately, she went into action and called 911 and my sister, Gennie, to let my family know what happened and that they needed to come to the hospital. I stayed in San Joaquin Hospital for a week before I was transferred to Healthsouth Rehabilitation Hospital for three weeks before I went home.

Let me tell you that this wasn't the beginning of my personal Job experience. It began years before. That will be discussed in another book. Before the stroke happened, I was already seeing a gynecologist for excessive bleeding every month. After several tests and an ultrasound, I was told that I had multiple fibroid tumors and the largest one was the size of a small watermelon.

Imagine that! A small watermelon. The doctor said that it was like being five months pregnant. I couldn't believe what I was hearing! After receiving that news, the stroke happened about two weeks later. Now, let's pick up where I left off with the stroke. I was in the rehabilitation hospital for approximately three weeks before I went home in January 2012.

I remember being so sad and depressed because I had to spend Christmas 2011 and New Year's Day 2012 in the hospital. Meanwhile, I was still trying to process what happened to me and why. At the time of my stroke, I was a self-employed business owner for seven years, and the next year was on target to be a bumper crop year. I couldn't believe it! Just like that, everything shut down. I told my niece, Breanna, "God should have just let me die!" She started crying and said, "Aunt Vicky don't say that. We got you." Then, she gave me a big hug. I was staying in my sister Loretta's home by then. Although I had that debilitating stroke, I was still having excessive bleeding every month because of the fibroids. My gynecologist called me and said that because it had been over a year since she last examined me, I needed to come in as soon as possible. I went to that appointment and was scheduled for a colposcopy with a biopsy. Ouch!

Get this picture. Because I am paralyzed on my left side, every time I need to have a major medical procedure, it has to be done in an operating room, and I have to be transferred on a gurney from my bed, and then taken to the hospital for the procedure. What a process! After the colposcopy was completed, I finally got back home after waiting several hours for the medical transportation van. It took them so long I told my sister, Patricia, to ask them to admit me to the hospital. What an ordeal! Several weeks later, the results of the biopsy showed Stage 1 cervical cancer. My doctor said that I had to have a total hysterectomy. I agreed because I knew at this point in my life, I would never give birth to biological children anyway. I wanted to have children when I was younger, but I understand now that wasn't in His plan for me. I'm an Isaiah 54:1 woman. Hallelujah!

So, on December 19, 2012, I had a total hysterectomy only

Vicky L. Richardson

two months after we laid my father to rest and just one year after I had a major stroke. Not just a major stroke, but a life interrupting stroke. My life was completely turned upside down. Everything was out of order. I felt like I was on a Ferris wheel and a roller coaster at the same time! Have you ever felt like that? Well, after surgery, I was in the hospital for several days.

When I was discharged, I felt it was best for me to go to a facility for wound care instead of going back to my sister Loretta's house. My uncle, Robert, was already living in one, and I decided to go where he was. I thought at least we could keep each other company. I was transferred into that facility on December 22, 2012, only three days before Christmas. We were so happy to see each other! I was only there four days before I had to go back to the hospital. The nurses there hadn't called the facility doctor to order some of the medication I needed. I remember asking the nurse about my medication, and her reply was, "I'm not calling him now. It's Christmas, and he'll yell at me for calling him!" I was too weak to press the issue. I went to sleep.

The next morning, I woke up soaking wet from profusely sweating all night. I instinctively knew that something was very wrong with me! I got my cell phone and called my sister, Gennie. I told her about the sweating, and she asked me to feel the area where the wound vac was and to tell her how it felt. To my surprise that area was as hard as a rock and as hot as fire! I told her how it felt, and she immediately told me to hang up, and she would call me back. Gennie has nursing experience, and she knew what was happening to me. She called back in a few minutes and told me that she had already talked to the facility charge nurse, and I was being sent back to the hospital immediately. I was dying, and I didn't know it. I just knew something was very, very wrong, and I felt horrible!

When the ambulance arrived, to my surprise and great relief, one of the EMT's was my niece, Charnessa. She had no idea the call was for me. When she came into my room, I thought she was coming to visit me. Divine assignments! I believe God made sure she was at work that morning just for me. She was so calm and reassuring. She said, "Don't worry, Aunt Vicky;

my partner and I will take good care of you." They transferred me to the gurney and took me out of that room quickly. I was in the ambulance before I knew it. It seemed like we were at the hospital in five minutes, although I know it was a little longer than that. And I don't think she hit a bump in the road. That was the smoothest ride ever. I'm telling you; my niece drove that ambulance under the anointing of God. I know she was praying for me during that entire time.

That's why I called it a divine assignment. Think about it! Of all the EMT's that work for that company, my niece gets the call to come take me to the hospital. God used her to help save my life that day. Another divine assignment was that my sister, Gennie, was working that day too. I was taken to the hospital where she worked. She met me in the emergency room. At first, the doctors were only talking to my sisters about what was wrong with me. My gynecologist was called in, and she told me that the wound vac had to be removed, and it would hurt as she took the staples out. It felt like fire ants were biting me as the staples were being removed. Ouch!

Next, the ER doctor and the RN came in to insert and start an IV. While the doctor was talking to me, he let me know that he would have to insert a picc line into my neck for the IV because I needed the strongest antibiotics in my body. I would also need a blood transfusion. By that time, I was so tired I said, "Talk to my sisters and do what you have to do." I didn't even ask what was wrong with me. At that point, I didn't care. I just wanted it to be over! That was December 26, 2012.

I was in the ER for hours because the emergency room doctors and nurses were doing one thing, and my gynecologist and her assistant were dealing with the removal of the wound vac and the staples. They had to thoroughly clean the wound and pack it. By the way, because of the paralysis on my left side, I had to have an abdominal hysterectomy. My abdomen still has a scar underneath my navel about an inch long where I was cut open. My gynecologist, Dr. Melissa Larsen, was the chief of obstetrics and gynecology at that same hospital. Divine assignments!

She and the emergency room doctors and nurses were

outstanding. After several hours in the emergency room, I was transferred upstairs to the ICU. I found out later that the doctors told my family that I had a blood infection called sepsis. They had only given me a fifty-fifty chance to live. I had five blood transfusions in addition to the strongest antibiotics you can receive. I remember the color of the antibiotics in the IV bag was brown. I asked the nurse, "What's that brown stuff?" She said, "That's your antibiotics." I said, "I have never seen any antibiotic like that." She said, "Miss Richardson, you are very sick, and this will help you get better. You need this."

I spent another week in the hospital. This time in the ICU. I celebrated New Year's 2013 at Kern Medical Center. On Wednesday, January 3, 2013, I was discharged to a different facility because my doctor refused to let me return to the one where my uncle lived. I had defeated death another year. To God be the glory! Hallelujah! Death had touched me several times between December 2011 and January 2013, but it could not take me. Glory to God! Hallelujah! Some of you reading this book may have your own testimony about death touching

You Can Live Through It: A Life Interrupted

you but not taking you.

Vicky L. Richardson

Chapter 2 Reflections

Use this page to write down your thoughts. Did this chapter help you? If so, how?

_____

_____

_____

_____

_____

_____

_____

It Hurt Me, But It Helped Me!

"Many are the afflictions of the righteous: but the Lord delivereth him out of them all" (Psalm 34:19, KJV).

Afflictions are normally an unwelcome event in our lives. Don't you agree? Affliction is something that causes pain or suffering to one's mental, emotional, or physical state. I don't welcome afflictions. I definitely didn't welcome this one. But I'm not going to avoid what I should learn during this process. Now, I realize the growth that I've achieved while going through this is imperative to the maturity that will be required in the next level of my life.

It's to one's advantage to learn the lesson that comes along with affliction during the process of going through it because it can be used to strengthen us and prepare us for a new dimension in our lives that will come after victoriously going through the present circumstance.

Therefore, you should gain more knowledge, wisdom, and compassion for other people during this season. When you go through affliction, you should be gaining something not losing something. An exchange should occur during times and seasons of affliction. For example, when Jesus was in the Garden of Gethsemane, He experienced mental and emotional affliction because He had second thoughts about what He was getting ready to physically go through.

Jesus gained something for us so that we could be delivered out of darkness. There should be an exchange made within the healing process of overcoming afflictions. The exchange made often includes an instruction or instructions to follow once you are delivered out of your affliction. For example, in John 5:14,

Jesus instructed the man healed of his affliction at the pool of Bethesda to stop sinning or something worse would happen to him. The affliction was removed, but the instruction to him remained.

For years, I watched my beautiful parents suffer daily with their afflictions. It hurt me to the deepest part of my soul to see them afflicted with so much pain. These questions lingered in my mind, "Why does God allow affliction into our lives? Why does a loving father permit so much pain and suffering in the lives of his children?" When going through affliction, you might wonder if He really loves you. Is He really good all the time as we say He is? If so, why am I hurting so badly? Lord knows when I started going through this affliction, I asked those questions and many more! You may have asked similar questions too. The answer is found in Psalm 119:71-72.

My mother read her Bible every morning she woke up and every night before she went to sleep. These two scriptures carried her through the numerous afflictions she endured. The first time I saw Psalm 119:71-72 was when my mother called me over to turn the pages for her because the arthritis in her hands was hurting too badly. Then I read it to her. Not because she asked me to but just because I wanted to. It actually seemed to help her feel better.

When I finished reading the verses she said, "Baby, God gave me these two scriptures when I was a young wife, and we lived in the projects. That was way before you were born. Your daddy and I were having a hard time in those days. I was so depressed that I was crawling on the floor crying, and I had three little girls to raise. I heard the Spirit tell me, 'Get up off that floor crying and get your Bible!' I got up and got my Bible, then it fell open to these scriptures. The Spirit said, 'Read it day and night for the rest of your life! I haven't missed a day. If I couldn't read my Bible for some reason, I quoted it from memory. And I will continue to do so as long as I am conscious."

I witnessed this word carry her through some of the darkest days of her life. She was covered with grace to go through her season of affliction. And so are you! You have been graced for this moment in your life. HALLELUJAH! She planted a seed in me that night when she asked me to help her turn those pages in her Bible. I have never forgotten Psalm 119:71 and it has carried me through some of the darkest days of my life. Thank you, Mama! Here's the answer to why affliction is allowed into the life of the believer.

"It is good for me that I have been afflicted, That I may learn Your statutes. The law from Your mouth is better to me Than thousands of gold and silver pieces" (Psalm 119:71-72, AMP).

The discipline and righteous character that God's Word teaches us is better than being the wealthiest person on Earth. Hallelujah! Think about that. The Word from the mouth of God is better than having as much money as Bill Gates.

The discipline from His Word is what gives us the strength to endure hardship or affliction as a good soldier of Jesus Christ (2 Timothy 2:3, KJV). It hurt me, but it helped me. That's why He said it is good for me that I have been afflicted! Why is it good? So, I may learn your statutes or that I may learn your laws. The laws of God are His Word. Hallelujah! Psalm 119:105 in the King James Version says, "Thy word is a lamp unto my feet, and a light unto my path."

You may be wondering how this affliction helped in my life? The first thought that comes to my mind is that it has shown me that I am stronger than I ever thought. The second thought is that my relationship with Jesus has grown exponentially over the past ten years. Am I perfect? Absolutely not! But I'm better. I refer to Philippians 3:14, "I press toward the goal for the prize of the upward call of God in Christ Jesus" (NKJV). The third thought is this. This affliction has allowed me to experience God's love in a way I hadn't before. There have been days that I have literally only thought about something I wanted and within a few hours or days I had it! One memory that sticks out for me is the day I had a fleeting thought about an Edible Arrangement. Within two hours, I received a surprise from my sister, Patricia, and it was an Edible Arrangement! The card said, "I was just thinking about you. Have a blessed day. Love Pat."

I realized God loves me so much that He cares about the little things I care about. I have so many examples like this. I call them God's special surprises. There are surprises and then there are SPECIAL surprises!

So, that's how this affliction has helped me. Let's briefly recap:

1. It has shown me I'm stronger than I thought I was.

2. My relationship with Jesus has grown exponentially.

3. I've experienced God's love in a new way.

This affliction has indeed hurt me in so many ways, but it has helped me so much more. As Mama used to say, "I wouldn't give anything for my journey now!" Glory, hallelujah!

Vicky L. Richardson

Chapter 3 Reflections

Use this page to write down your thoughts. Did this chapter help you? If so, how?

_____

_____

_____

_____

_____

_____

_____

There's A Purpose In Your Pause

"Listen carefully, I am about to do a new thing, Now it will spring forth; Will you not be aware of it? I will even put a road in the wilderness, Rivers in the desert" (Isaiah 43:19, AMP).

"And He who sits on the throne said, "Behold, I am making all things new." Also, He said, "Write, for these words are faithful and true [they are accurate, incorruptible, and trustworthy]" (Revelation 21:5, AMP).

Some of us have been on pause in life, and it looks like an absolute end has occurred. The good news is it's only temporary!

To pause:

a temporary stop.

Temporary:

lasting for a limited time.

Ecclesiastes 3:1 (KJV) says, "To every thing there is a season, and a time to every purpose under heaven."

Sometimes, God has to press the reset button on our lives. When that happens, it may seem as though your life has stopped, and it has for a little while. Your old life has stopped. Life as you knew it is now obsolete. God has pressed the reset button on your life. At first, fear will try to intimidate you, then anger will try to blind you. Then depression will try to keep you immobile. These are all weights. Fear, anger, depression. Lay them aside and embrace the reset.

"Wherefore seeing we also are compassed about with so great a cloud of witnesses, let us lay aside every weight, and the sin which doth so easily beset us, and let us run with patience the race that is set before us,"

(Hebrews 12:1, KJV).

At times, it will feel like you're being left behind and that life is passing you by. But the fact of the matter is, you are being prepared for God to catapult you far ahead when he pushes the reset button. 5, 4, 3, 2, 1, 0… Blast off! Don't despise the fact that God has pushed the reset button on your life. It's in His plan for your life and it's for your own good!

"And we know that all things work together for good to them that love God, to them who are the called according to his purpose" (Romans 8:28, KJV).

Embrace the reset in your life! This time of reset is more necessary and valuable than you realize. Take a deep breath, relax, and rest. Before I was afflicted by the stroke, I was a workaholic. I didn't know how to rest.

Vicky L. Richardson

Chapter 4 Reflections

Use this page to write down your thoughts. Did this chapter help you? If so, how?

_____

_____

_____

_____

_____

_____

_____

Rest In The Reset

The word rest is also found in the word reset. In this season where your life has been interrupted, the rest that you are getting while on reset will be much appreciated. I have come to appreciate every bit of the rest that I have been getting during this time of my life.

The reset button was also pressed on the life of Job. When his power button was finally pushed, he received double the blessings that he had before. Not only was he a better man, a better person, but he also had a better understanding of who he was and more importantly of who God was!

We know this because when he complained to God about his situation, God replied in a way that made Job thoroughly understand who God was. In Job 38:4, God asked him this question, "Where were you when I laid the foundation of the earth?" And He didn't stop there. The entire thirty-eighth chapter is God asking Job questions about His sovereignty that left him speechless.

Although he complained about some of the things he did not understand, God didn't hold it against him. Honestly, I've had days when I complained to God too, and He brought me back to my right mind just like He did Job. Hallelujah! Not only did Job's possessions increase, but his knowledge, wisdom, and understanding increased.

"And the Lord turned the captivity of Job, when he prayed for his friends; also the Lord gave Job twice as much as he had before. Then came there unto him all his brethren, and all his sisters, and all they that had been of his acquaintance before, and did eat bread with him in his house; and they bemoaned him, and comforted him over all the evil that the Lord had brought upon him; every man also gave him a piece of money, and every one an earring of gold. So the Lord blessed the latter end of Job more than his beginning, for he had fourteen thousand sheep; and six thousand camels; and a thousand yoke of oxen, and a thousand she asses"

(Job 42:10-12, KJV).

Your pause in life is coming to an end... soon. Say this, "There is a purpose in my pause!" Your pause is only for a season. Seasons not only change. but they also come to an end. Isn't that great news? Let's reread Jeremiah 29:11: "For I know the plans I have for you, declares the Lord, plans to prosper you and not to harm you, to give you a hope and a future." Plans, pauses, purposes! There is a purpose in your pause, and it has everything to do with His plan for your life, not your plan, but His plan. His plans are sure and eternal. He has a forever plan designed just for you. That's why He said to give you hope and a future.

Think about that... hope and a future! Your pause is soon

coming to an end. Your season is changing. Some of you have been on pause for so long that you should be ready to hit the ground running. I know I sure am. Glory hallelujah! By now, you should have learned the lesson God was teaching you. By now, you should be so fed up with sin and its results that you could stomp Satan into the ground. By now, you should know yourself so much better. By now, you should know who can and cannot be in your inner circle. By now, you should know who your friends are and those people who are not.

By now, your eyes should be wide open. By now, you should be so fed up with foolishness. By now, you should be ready to serve God for real. These are the last of the last days. Are you really ready? Don't answer that if you're not ready.

Remember, there's a purpose in your pause! You could say, "There's a cause for the pause." How many of you reading this book have been on pause in your life? I'll raise my hand first!

Job worshipped when adversity interrupted his life. He had a come-what-may attitude. That's precisely the kind of attitude that it takes to endure a major life interruption. That kind of attitude says, "Whatever comes, whatever happens, or doesn't happen, I will still love God. I will still worship and praise him." Hallelujah! This is the attitude that overcomes adversity.

"Job stood up and tore his robe in grief. Then he shaved his head and fell to the ground to worship. He said, "I came naked from my mother's womb, and I will be naked when I leave. The Lord gave me what I had, and the Lord has taken away. Praise the name of the Lord!" In all of this, Job did not sin by blaming God" (Job 1:20-22, NLT).

The attitude that overcomes adversity is one that assumes the posture of worship when everything in your life is falling apart and has been severely interrupted. Verse twenty above says Job fell to the ground and worshipped when he received all that disturbing news. Let's take a moment and read what actually happened to Job before verse twenty.

"One day when Job's sons and daughters were feasting at the oldest brother's house, a messenger arrived at Job's home with this news: "Your oxen were plowing with the donkeys feeding beside them, when the Sabeans raided us. They stole all the animals and killed all the farmhands. I am the only one who escaped to tell you." While he was still speaking, another messenger arrived with this news: "The fire of God has fallen from heaven and burned your sheep and all the shepherds. I am the only one who escaped to tell you." While he was still speaking, a thief messenger arrived with this news: "Three bands of Chaldean raiders have stolen your camels and killed your servants. I am the only one who escaped to tell you." While he was still speaking, another messenger arrived with this news: "Your sons and daughters were feasting in their oldest brother's home. Suddenly, a powerful wind swept in from the wilderness and hit the house on all sides. The house collapsed, and all your children are dead. I am the only one who escaped to tell you."

These things happened to him one right after the other! Job could not even catch his breath and gather his thoughts from receiving so much back-to-back devastating news. The only appropriate response he knew was to worship during his crisis.

It's imperative that we model his example whenever we find ourselves in a major crisis. Within the last month, while writing this book, I had to do exactly what I am telling you to do. I have suffered another outbreak of shingles, and this time, the scars that they left have been extremely painful. I had to take some time off before I could finish writing this book. I was empty, completely drained. I could not think of anything else to write after going through shingles this time. At least that's what I thought. But as you can see, I still have more left inside of me to write.

Physical adversity, mental adversity, emotional adversity, societal adversity, financial adversity. and spiritual adversity have all come at some point. Through it all, God gave Job sustainable grace to endure his testing. I am experiencing that same sustainable grace right now to endure the greatest test of my life. I pray that you will also experience the sustainable grace of God when you need it.

"But we have this treasure in earthen vessels, that the excellency of the power may be of God, and not of us. We are troubled on every side, yet not distressed; we are perplexed, but not in despair;

Vicky L. Richardson

Persecuted, but not forsaken; cast down, but not destroyed; Always bearing about in the body the dying of the Lord Jesus, that the life also of Jesus might be made manifest in our body" (2 Corinthians 4:7-10, KJV).

You Can Live Through It: A Life Interrupted

Chapter 5 Reflections

Use this page to write down your thoughts. Did this chapter help you? If so, how?

_____

_____

_____

_____

_____

_____

_____

Life As I Knew It: The Acceptance

I have learned that "acceptance is not submission." Acceptance can be submission. Before this stroke happened to me, I thought submission meant that I was mentally and emotionally weaker than what I was submitting to. Eventually, I came to realize that acceptance of my new reality because of this life interruption did not make me weak at all! Rather, this acceptance made me stronger. Once I realized this. I stopped avoiding my new life. I embraced it!

"Acceptance is not submission; it is acknowledgement of

You Can Live Through It: A Life Interrupted

the facts of the situation. Then deciding what you're going to do about it." ~Kathleen Casey Theisen

Acceptance versus Avoidance

Acceptance acknowledges that now I must use a wheelchair and that I live in a residential care facility. This is my new home and new community. I will make new friends. This is still my life and I have a new way of living it. Therefore, I choose to get the best out of this life interruption.

"Interruptions: They're aggravating; sometimes infuriating. They make us want to tell people what we think of them. But how we handle interruptions actually tells us more about ourselves."

~Priscilla Shirer (Life Interrupted)

Vicky L. Richardson

Chapter 6 Reflections

Use this page to write down your thoughts. Did this chapter help you? If so, how?

_____

_____

_____

_____

_____

_____

_____

My Life Isn't Over Yet

I learned that I had the option to live in the past, or I could make the decision to keep going and make my life as great as it can be now.

I'm having an amazing life. And it isn't over yet. How do I know? I'm glad you asked that question! I hosted and was the mistress of ceremony for an elegant hat fashion show in the facility I live in... all done from my wheelchair! Some of the residents were the models in their wheelchairs, and it was an absolutely amazing event. It was the first one ever done in this facility. We modeled some of the most beautiful hats ever made for women, and that's not all. I was also the resident pastor here from 2014-2017. That is another first in this facility. We had church service almost every Sunday. After a necessary break due to a health crisis, I resumed having Sunday services with the residents this year in 2021.

You can discover what you can still do and contribute to enhance another person's life while enhancing yours at the same time. Your life is not over yet. Don't put a period where God only placed a comma. *You Can Live Through It!*

I admit that initially I had placed a period on my life after I had the stroke. I thought I was finished. Writing those words just made me laugh. I am actually writing a book about my life! And I thought I was finished. As mentioned earlier, I had to take a break. Now, I am writing again, but slowly. This recent bout with shingles took a lot of energy from me. I am fifty-three years old now, and I have to admit that the recovery from things like this takes a little longer than it used to. I hate satan. I don't even like to capitalize his name. I was in a serious flow. Now,

You Can Live Through It: A Life Interrupted

I find myself struggling to get back there, but I have faith that is beyond my reality. I shall overcome. Hallelujah and to God be the glory!

"For which cause we faint not; but though our outward man perish, yet the inward man is renewed day by day" (2 Corinthians 4:16, KJV).

The goal is for you to discover that your life can still be fun, fulfilling, and fabulous even though you have experienced a major life interruption. There is more inside of you left to give to the world!

"Honestly, it is when one is raw and real and truthful that healing can begin. And in that place of exposing, one's life does it allow others to feel the bravery to talk about THEIR lives without hiding behind the cloak of fear, shame, or not feeling valued." ~Rachel Marie Martin

From the website: http://findingjoy.net/when-life-isnt-what-you-thought

Vicky L. Richardson

Chapter 7 Reflections

Use this page to write down your thoughts. Did this chapter help you? If so, how?

_____

_____

_____

_____

_____

_____

_____

_____

I Miss You, The Grieving Process

I have also learned that grief isn't only experienced when you lose a loved one, but the grieving process can be experienced whenever you suffer a loss of any kind, such as a loss of your independence. Then there's the loss of being with your family and friends regularly in familiar surroundings. The loss of your identity, meaning who or what you were known as before your life was interrupted can cause us to grieve.

I found reading 15 Things I Wish I'd Known About Grief by Teryn O'Brien to be very helpful for me, particularly numbers one and ten.

I will paraphrase them here. You will feel like the world has ended. But it hasn't. Life will continue. A new normal will come, slowly. It's important to face grief. Rather than to hide from the pain. If not, you will become bitter and cynical. You must face it. Your life has been interrupted, but it is not over yet. *You Can Live Through It!*

I also learned the importance of giving yourself permission to grieve, letting go of the past, and moving forward into a promising future.

I gave myself permission to grieve the loss of life as I knew it. Allowing myself to mourn the loss of my independence gave me the emotional space I needed to heal and move on with my new life.

"Imagine a new story for your life and start living it."-Paulo Coelho

You Can Live Through It: A Life Interrupted

Chapter 8 Reflections

Use this page to write down your thoughts. Did this chapter help you? If so, how?

_____

_____

_____

_____

_____

_____

_____

Unshakeable Faith

"But without faith it is impossible to please him: for he that cometh to God must believe that he is, and that he is a rewarder of them that diligently seek him" (Hebrews 11:6, KJV).

I thought June 7, 2010, was the darkest day of my life. That was the day my beautiful mother unexpectedly died. I was completely devastated and felt the weight of my whole family on my shoulders. How could I ever carry them through this? What they didn't know was that she had asked me to be the peacemaker in the family after she wasn't here anymore. When she left us, I was an emotional wreck! How in the world could I be the peacemaker in the family when I was so angry with God? Little by little that anger left. I cried out to Him like I never had before. There were other times when I cried out to God, but this was different. My mama was gone! I sent up a wailing cry. I'm so thankful that He heard me. Every day I let God hold me closer and tighter until I became overwhelmed by His unfailing love. Hallelujah!

That allowed me to have the faith I needed to carry them through the darkest days of our lives as a family. I knew they were watching me and depending on me to help them get through this. Although at the time, they may not have realized it. I knew I couldn't break down. Even though I am the youngest of my siblings, like King David and Joseph, God made me different. I had an undeniable anointing on my life. I call it the Anointing of the Last Born.

Just like David and Joseph needed unshakeable faith to help them complete the specific assignments God had given them, I needed that same unshakeable faith. Hallelujah!

God has created us to be unstoppable! For us to be unstoppable, we must have unshakeable faith. What is unstoppable and unshakeable faith? It is a faith that is so focused and anchored in God and His Word that there is no room for doubt to creep in! That's why David was absolutely convinced that he could take Goliath out. Unshakeable faith is what carried Joseph all the way from the pit to the palace! Glory hallelujah! That is a relentless faith... a faith that just keeps on going. A faith that keeps believing. A faith that never gives up. Relentless and unshakable faith. Hallelujah! Relentless faith is the most important component for us to be unshakeable and unstoppable.

"Now faith is the substance of things hoped for, the evidence of things not seen" (Hebrews 11:1, KJV).

You Can Live Through It: A Life Interrupted

Chapter 9 Reflections

Use this page to write down your thoughts. Did this chapter help you? If so, how?

_____

_____

_____

_____

_____

_____

_____

Trials and Tribulations

The Importance of Having the Right Attitude and Perspective

"Consider it pure joy, my brothers and sisters, whenever you face trials of many kinds, because you know that the testing of your faith produces perseverance. Let perseverance finish its work so that you may be mature and complete, not lacking anything. If any of you lacks wisdom, you should ask God, who gives generously to all without finding fault, and it will be given to you. But when you ask, you must believe and not doubt, because the one who doubts is like a wave of the sea, blown and tossed by the wind. That person should not expect to receive anything from the Lord. Such a person is double-minded and unstable in all they do" (James 1:2-8, NIV).

We're talking about being unstoppable during our trials and tribulations.

Point 1- You must have unshakeable and relentless faith.

Point 2- You must have a positive attitude and perspective.

Reread verses five and six above and let's thoroughly examine them.

Verse five says, "If any of you lacks wisdom, you should ask God." When we go through trials and tribulations, we absolutely need wisdom to understand how to endure them until we get through them. Hallelujah! We get this wisdom from him by asking questions, and he teaches us and encourages us to continue to glorify him and worship him while we are waiting for our deliverance out of these afflictions. Hallelujah!

Sidebar: When I was a child, we were taught that you don't ask God questions. Was anyone else taught that? Well, I'm telling you that belief is incorrect! I believe that the thought process of not questioning God came about because of the rebuke Job received when he complained to God about the testing he was going through. Beloved, there's a vast difference between complaining to God about what you're going through and asking questions to get a better understanding of why you have to go through it in the first place.

Jesus even questioned God. In Matthew 26:39, He didn't phrase it as a question, but the implication is strongly stated. The scripture says this, "And he went a little farther, and fell on his face, and prayed, saying, O my Father, if it be possible, let this cup pass from me: nevertheless, not as I will, but as thou wilt." In other words, Jesus was asking the Father, "Do I really have to do this? Is it possible to do this another way?"

So, clearly, we can ask God questions. Maybe just not phrase them as questions.

While I have been going through this testing, I have asked God a lot of questions to get a better understanding of why I was chosen for this trial. He answered some of my questions, and others He didn't. And that's when I said to Him what Jesus said. "Nevertheless not my will, but your will be done" in and through my life. Amen!

When you doubt the Word of God, it is easy for you to become double-minded, fickle, or tossed around in your thoughts. You begin to have stinking thinking. Just like the waves of the ocean, you will start drifting off course like a ship lost at sea. Believe the Word of God. Believe the Bible. Doubt cancels the request. You don't want to be like that person. You want to be unstoppable, not unstable. Repeat after me: Lord help me to be an unstoppable Christian, not an unstable Christian.

"Ask, and it shall be given you; seek, and ye shall find; knock, and it shall be opened unto you:

For every one that asketh receiveth; and he that seeketh findeth; and to him that knocketh it shall be opened"

(Matthew 7:7-8, KJV).

Satan may knock you down, but he cannot knock you out. Why not? Romans 16:20 declares, "And the God of peace will crush Satan under your feet shortly." Hallelujah! Hold on, a change is coming.

You are unstoppable. Although you've had a life interruption, *you can live through it!*

Father, I pray that everyone who reads this book will receive the strength and sustainable grace they need to endure the darkest days of their lives and to live through this life interruption. In Jesus' name. Amen.

You Can Live Through It: A Life Interrupted

Chapter 10 Reflections

Use this page to write down your thoughts. Did this chapter help you? If so, how?

_____

_____

_____

_____

_____

_____

_____

Navigating Through The Unexpected

Many people have an idea or a goal in mind of where they would like their lives to be or what they want to have accomplished in life if they are blessed to live to forty and beyond. But some of them do not have an alternate plan if some catastrophic events were to happen. And how would they navigate through such an unexpected occurrence? I sure didn't. I was so focused on building my business that I had never considered what if something happened to me and I could not work anymore?

After all, I was in my early forties and working on my plan to be successful.

"To appoint unto them that mourn in Zion, to give unto them beauty for ashes, the oil of joy for mourning, the garment of praise for the spirit of heaviness, that they might be called trees of righteousness, the planting of the Lord, that He might be glorified" (Isaiah 61:3, KJV).

I have two questions for you. Number one is what have you done or what are you doing to navigate through the unexpected in your life? Question number two is have you given thought to how you can navigate through the unexpected if you haven't already? As I mentioned earlier in this book, navigating through the unexpected has been quite the experience for me. My navigation began with embracing my life as it is now. I had to accept that the lifestyle I previously enjoyed was gone. Before my unexpected interruption, I wore many hats. I was a musician for the majority of my previous life, and because the stroke left half of my body paralyzed, I can no longer play the musical instruments I fell in love with. Those are the piano, organ, and the drums.

Vicky L. Richardson

I played the drums professionally for thirteen years and was blessed to travel nationwide. I was blessed to play for some of gospel music's most notable artists, such as Evangelist Beverly Crawford, Dr. Bobby Jones, Evangelist Dorothy Norwood, Pastor Sheryl Brady, and Phil Driscoll to name a few.

It took a while for me to enjoy listening to music again. It was a constant reminder of what had been stolen from me. So, I just refused to turn it on. I remember my sister, Gennie, playing a song by Marvin Sapp one afternoon, and I started sobbing uncontrollably. I just didn't want to hear music AT ALL! But my family knew how much I dearly loved it, so they kept playing it through videos, CDs and DVDs. One day, my sister, Patricia, came into my room with a DVD player and a lot of CDs and DVDs. She didn't know it, but I wanted to throw everything she brought in there right out of the window! I didn't realize it at the time, but they were helping me navigate through the unexpected whether I wanted them to or not. I'm so glad they kept being the sometimes irritating, won't take no for an answer, big sisters that they always were when we were kids, especially

Patricia. But everything they did for me was strictly from the deep love and respect they have for me and the innate sense of protection that big sisters have for little sisters. I believe they could clearly see that my will to overcome was gone.

Before I knew it, I was enjoying music again. Hallelujah! I thank God for my family. I had forgotten Isaiah 61:3, but they hadn't. Honestly, at that point, I didn't care to remember it. I was a mess. I wanted to give up on God, but He wouldn't let me go, and I'm so happy that He didn't. I had to continually listen not only to kingdom music but also the Word of God.

I had to eat His food daily just like I ate my natural food daily. During that time, not only had I lost my appetite for natural food, but I had also lost my appetite for the Word. I've come to realize that in those days, I felt completely betrayed by God. Doesn't that sound crazy? I was for a little while. That's what life interruptions can do to you. They can get you completely off track with sober thinking. Listening to gospel music and the Word of God got me back to sober thinking.

"Let this mind be in you, which was also in Christ Jesus"

(Philippians 2:5, KJV).

Navigating through the unexpected will most certainly require you having the mind of Jesus Christ in you. You may wonder how I navigate the unexpected while living inside of a skilled nursing facility. I mentioned a few things in the beginning of this book, but that's not nearly all. In 2016, I taught an eight-week class called "Life Interrupted" to the residents who lived here then. It was the first of its kind in this facility but a great success. I give God all of the glory for blessing me to complete that assignment. In fact, those classes, along with several sermons I have preached while having Sunday services here are what birthed the title of this book, You Can Live Through It.

It's imperative that you continue to do some of the things you can still do and enjoy doing before your life interruption. That's how you begin the process of navigating through the unexpected. It takes a lot more effort now for me to do some of the things I enjoyed before. I may not do them as often, but I still do them. That's how I continue to navigate through this new life. And I feel great whenever I do. Easter Sunday in 2021,

I left the facility to go see my family after having been locked inside for over a year because of Covid-19. It wasn't an easy process, but I did what I had to do because I wanted to see my family without the separation of a window. Believe me when I tell you that satan tried everything he could to keep me from leaving the facility and spending time with them, but it did not work. Hallelujah! Repeat after me: "I still have value! I will victoriously navigate this unexpected interruption!"

Vicky L. Richardson

Chapter 11 Reflections

Use this page to write down your thoughts. Did this chapter help you? If so, how?

_____

_____

_____

_____

_____

_____

_____

I Thank God For Yesterday

I've heard some people say to leave yesterday alone. Because it's in the past and there isn't anything that's good about it. Sometimes that's true. But for me it is not. I have found that yesterday was a great day. Was it perfect? No, it wasn't. Because I wasn't perfect. Like the Apostle Paul, I had a lot to learn, and I still do.

"I don't mean to say I am perfect. I haven't learned all I should even yet, but I keep working toward that day when I will finally be all that Christ saved me for and wants me to be.

Vicky L. Richardson

No, dear brothers, I am still not all I should be, but I am bringing all my energies to bear on this one thing: Forgetting the past and looking forward to what lies ahead, I strain to reach the end of the race and receive the prize for which God is calling us up to heaven because of what Christ Jesus did for us" (Philippians 32:12-14, TLB).

I posted this to my Facebook page on April 26, 2021. This is one of the pictures I found while going through my phone recently. When I first saw it, I gasped and slightly turned away.

Then the Holy Spirit said, "Look at the picture!" I did, and to my pleasant surprise, I loved it!

I started looking at my family members and remembering what this occasion was. It was my father's birthday party. Next, I looked at myself, standing and using both of my hands! I was taking a picture of my nephew, Tyson, who was only one year old. Then I stared at myself and how beautiful I was that day.

I was remembering how much fun we had celebrating my dad. The longer I looked at this picture the more I thanked God for yesterday. Gospel artist, Mary Mary, had a hit song entitled "Yesterday." It was my dad's favorite song. He had been living through his own life interruption for about thirteen years when this picture was taken. He was also afflicted by the same kind of stroke that I had. I remember Daddy would listen to "Yesterday" and cry and praise God.

There's a line in the song that says, "I cried my last tear yesterday." When I examined this picture, I also started crying and thanking God for yesterday. I understood that Daddy wasn't saddened by this song. To the contrary, it made him happy. His tears were tears of joy. Because he had already cried his last tear about losing his independence yesterday. Glory to God! Hallelujah!

When I saw this picture, I finally understood exactly what Daddy meant when he said, "I cried my last tear yesterday. I'm not going to worry about it anymore." He was free. Now, I'm free.

Free from what? Free from carrying the weight of depression. Free from feeling sorry for myself. Free from being angry with God. Free from feeling like life has left me behind. Free from feeling embarrassed about what has happened to me. Free from wondering what people are saying or thinking about what has happened to me. Hallelujah, I am free!

I thank God for yesterday because I reconciled with my soul. The soul consists of the mind, the will, and the emotions. Remember the last line of the song says, "I cried my last tear yesterday."

Let's examine what I just said. I reconciled with my soul. Here's the definition of reconciled from the Oxford Language Dictionary:

You Can Live Through It: A Life Interrupted

"Restore friendly relations between. Cause to coexist in harmony; make or show to be compatible."

That means that yesterday my soul was perplexed and out of sync with the will of God for my life. My mind was disturbed, my will was in rebellion, and my emotions were unstable. But yesterday, I reconciled with my soul. Glory hallelujah! I thank God for yesterday.

Vicky L. Richardson

Chapter 12 Reflections

Use this page to write down your thoughts. Did this chapter help you? If so, how?

_____

_____

_____

_____

_____

_____

_____

Embracing Your Life Now: The Identity Crisis

"I praise you, for I am fearfully and wonderfully made. Wonderful are your works; my soul knows it very well" (Psalm 139:14, ESV).

The following is from a handout that I gave to residents during the "Life Interrupted" classes that I mentioned previously. I believe that it will help those of you reading this book who are now learning how to live through your own life interruptions.

Vicky L. Richardson

You may not be in a wheelchair, but whatever has happened in your life that caused the title of my book to interest you is your wheelchair for the purpose of this chapter.

Who am I now? How do I redefine myself? I don't recognize who I am. Will anyone else? These are just a few of the many questions that will arise during an identity crisis. Well, here is the answer to those questions. What you did in your life before the interruption did not define who you were as a person. Who you are inside defines you.

Contrary to popular belief your job was not your identity. Neither is the role you played in life, such as homemaker, social club president, or whatever you did to earn a living that satisfied the place inside of you before this abrupt change occurred.

Rather, your identity is defined by your character. The real you! You know the person who looks back at you when looking into a mirror. Here's some great news: The same person that sat inside of the car who drove to and from work daily is the same person right now. I repeat, your occupation did not define you. What's on the inside defines you. Who you were then is

You Can Live Through It: A Life Interrupted

who you are now.

You are still you! A wheelchair only changes who you are as a person if you allow it to. Don't let the chair tell you who you are or are not.

Make this declaration for yourself. "I am who I am. I am still (insert your name). I will not let this interruption change who I am. Rather, I will allow it to make me better, not bitter. I will embrace my life as it is now."

Vicky L. Richardson

Chapter 13 Reflections

Use this page to write down your thoughts. Did this chapter help you? If so, how?

_____

_____

_____

_____

_____

_____

_____

The Life We Leave Behind

"No, dear brothers, I am still not all I should be, but I am bringing all my energies to bear on this one thing: Forgetting the past and looking forward to what lies ahead," (Philippians 3:13, TLB).

Giving up the life you planned is not easy. In fact, leaving your old life behind may be the hardest thing you will ever do. It sure has been for me. But it has also been a very rewarding experience for me. Letting go of the old to embrace the new, realizing that what I thought was an ending was really an amazing beginning.

Giving up the life you knew and were accustomed to isn't just about walking away from a job that you loved to enter retirement or because you can no longer perform it due to declining health. Neither is it about losing a house that you dearly loved that was destroyed by a natural disaster.

It is also not about a marriage that has ended in divorce, and it definitely is not about being able to enjoy your favorite activity because the city or state is on lockdown because of Covid-19. Giving up the life you were acquainted with is also not about leaving behind dreams that you realize may not become reality now due to this major life interruption.

The life we leave behind is all about embracing a new you, a you that was undiscovered. It is all about a you that perhaps tried to emerge previously but was hindered by fear, doubt, or insecurity. It is also about exchanging your previous plans to become someone better now than you were then. This is exactly what I am experiencing now. The undiscovered person inside of me was Vicky L. Richardson, the author.

You Can Live Through It: A Life Interrupted

Chapter 14 Reflections

Use this page to write down your thoughts. Did this chapter help you? If so, how?

_____

_____

_____

_____

_____

_____

_____

Restructuring Your Purpose

How in the world can I ever restructure my purpose? I had to give some deep thought to this question. My purpose is to minister to the needs of others and to preach the Gospel of Jesus Christ.

Shortly after high school, I started ministering through music, traveling, and playing instruments for one of the groups or choirs I accompanied. I also sang and led the congregation in worship and praise every Sunday when I lived in Hanford, California. I had served in full-time ministry for the majority of my adult life. After things changed so drastically, I thought, "How will I continue to fulfill my purpose?" I couldn't play instruments anymore. I couldn't stand up to preach or sing anymore. Ah... but I could still do it!

I just had to restructure how I would fulfill my purpose. That process began on Sunday, June 8, 2014, when I led my first worship service here in the facility. I was singing, preaching, and ministering faithfully to the residents and whoever needed it each week for three years until I had a change in my health that required me having to take a break for a while. Shingles...what a very painful condition! And it takes a while to get over that.

When I got over them and was no longer confined to my room, I was so physically weak. I knew that I still wouldn't be able to have weekly services for a while longer, so I let it be known that my door was open for prayer and encouragement when needed. The residents and employees took advantage of the opportunity. Hallelujah!

When you are going through your own Job experience, it may require you to restructure your purpose multiple times. I had to go from weekly corporate worship services to one-on-one personal ministry, so I could continue to fulfill my purpose. In addition to full-time ministry in this facility, I also started a virtual ministry through social media in 2014. All of that has evolved into the writing of this book, my first book.

You Can Live Through It: A Life Interrupted

Chapter 15 Reflections

Use this page to write down your thoughts. Did this chapter help you? If so, how?

_____

_____

_____

_____

_____

_____

_____

Facebook Posts

I have a habit of saving some of my Facebook posts that were the most encouraging to those on my friends list throughout the years. As I read them, I realized they encouraged me too, not knowing that one day these posts, along with my experiences in life would become the foundation for this book.

Be encouraged tonight because there is glory in your story! You are not going through what you are going through for nothing. There is glory coming out of your story. Your life is a story. You know why? Because Jeremiah 29:11 (KJV) says, "For I know the thoughts that I think toward you, saith the Lord, thoughts of peace, and not of evil, to give you an expected end." The story of your life was written long long ago. God is the author of your life. Job 23:10 says, "But he knoweth the way that I take: when he hath tried me, I shall come forth as gold." That sounds like there's glory in your story to me! Have a blessed evening! Good night! Love to all!!!" Originally posted on Facebook March 3, 2015.

"Some things in life God will allow to touch you but not take you out. In other words, it won't kill you because it can't kill you! But it will touch you! No weapon formed against you shall prosper!" Originally Posted on Facebook May 5, 2014.

"While you are believing for and waiting on the biggest miracle of your life, God may require you to make an unexpected sacrifice. like when He asked Abraham for Isaac. Abraham was accustomed to making sacrifices on the altar but to be required to sacrifice his only son? When he obeyed God and tied Isaac to that altar, God told him to stay his hand. At that point, God knew Abraham honored Him! In fact, the text says in Genesis 22:12 that God said now I know you fear God! Can God say that of you? Now, I know that (insert your name) fears (honors) Me. Has God required an unexpected sacrifice of you? A song we rarely hear anymore is "Is your all on the altar of sacrifice." Youtube it and let it saturate your spirit. Now I know! I want God to say not only well done to me, but I also want Him to say now I know that Vicky honors me. Hallelujah!!!! Glorayyyyyy!!!" Originally posted on Facebook April 7, 2014

"The definition of order is the accurate arrangement of things. Now, keep in mind that when you pray and ask Yahweh to put something in order that you have become accustomed to being out of order, it will be dramatically shuffled around. And your life will appear to be much worse while Yahweh is rearranging things in your life so that He can arrange them in accurate order. That's why for a SHORT time, your life may get worse before it gets better. But do not despair! Yahweh is answering your prayer! Things are getting better! Romans 8:28(KJV) says, "And we know that all things work together for good to them that love God, to them who are the called according to his purpose." Be encouraged. He has answered your prayer!" Originally posted on Facebook March 12, 2014

Encouraging Scriptures

The following scriptures are what I call my 911 scriptures. They give me encouragement and strength to live through this life interruption. They bring me much comfort on tough days, and I pray they will do the same for you.

"I waited patiently for the Lord; and he inclined unto me, and heard my cry. He brought me up also out of an horrible pit, out of the miry clay, and set my feet upon a rock, and established my goings. And he hath put a new song in my mouth, even praise unto our God: many shall see it, and fear, and shall trust in the Lord" (Psalm 40:1-3, KJV).

"Cast not away therefore your confidence, which hath great recompence of reward. For ye have need of patience, that, after ye have done the will of God, ye might receive the promise. For yet a little while, and he that shall come will come, and will not tarry. Now the just shall live by faith: but if any man draw back, my soul shall have no pleasure in him" (Hebrews 10:35-38, KJV).

"Who in the days of his flesh, when he had offered up prayers and supplications with strong crying and tears unto him that was able to save him from death, and was heard in that he feared; Though he were a Son, yet learned he obedience by the things which he suffered" (Hebrews 3:7-8, KJV).

Works Cited

Martin, Rachel M. When Life Isn't What You Thought It Would Be. http://findingjoy.net/when-life-isnt-what-you-thought.

Mary Mary, "Yesterday," track #6 on Mary Mary, Columbia Records, 2005, compact disc.

O'Brien, Teryn. 2013, November 21. 15 Things I Wish I'd Known About Grief. Teryn O'Brien Art & Movement. http://terynobrien.com/healing/15thingsiwishidknownaboutgrief/.

Shirer, P. (2011). Life interrupted: Navigating the unexpected. B & H Pub.

If you were blessed by this book, please leave a book review on Amazon.